I0836962

THE UNIVERSITY OF MICHIGAN
·LIBRARIES·
THE UNIVERSITY OF MICHIGAN
1817

Glimpses of New York

Glimpses of New York

An Illustrated Handbook of the City, together with Notes on the Electric Industry therein and thereabout

Compiled and Edited by
The New York Edison Company

To the members of the National Electric Light Association, in convention assembled, May 30, 1911, this little Edison Baedeker of New York is respectfully dedicated.

In it, we shall try to show you our city—to us the most fascinating in the world. We love its skyscrapers and its tenements, its high finance and its subways, its fitful strivings after the good and the beautiful. The Great White Way and the little side streets, the polyglot speech of new peoples that throng our streets; splendor, squalor, commercialism, humanity, these are all New York.

And if in showing you our city, we can't help seeing electricity as the motive power of it all, you must pardon us; we are personally prejudiced.

Liberty Enlightening the World

Free-handed, our Sister Nation, France, gave her to America in eighteen hundred and eighty-six.

But strange it was, that when the gift arrived, no thought had been given to the receiving of it, and only through the prompt action of one of the city's patriotic newspapers, was the country finally awakened to its responsibility.

So, after twelve years of preparation, this colossal statue, conceived and designed by Monsieur Bartholdi, was unveiled on Bedloe's Island in the Harbor of New York.

Made of copper and steel, it weighs two hundred and twenty-five tons and reaches up over three hundred feet, to where the hand holds a powerful electric torch. Battered by many a hundred storms, she has stood at the foot of the bay for more than twenty years—and still is unafraid! She is watching, guarding new Children of the Republic as they come in from overseas.

The North River water front

From the Jersey Shore

The Singer Building towering over lower New York

Up-town from the Jersey Shore. Times Tower and the Metropolitan are the highest peaks

Singer and City Investment Buildings from the East River

Three East River Bridges

Ellis Island

Pause for a space, and watch the fascinating sight of a nation growing at the rate of three thousand people a day!

On this small island, are gathered up the threads of many-tongued humanity, from all the far corners of the Earth.

It is the melting-pot of the Republic; where every possible ingredient is fused into the larger metal of an American Citizen.

Pathos and Laughter, Sorrow and Gay Inconsequence, go trustfully together, seeking, with upturned faces, a new home, under the protecting arm of the great figure of Liberty.

Governors Island

Governors Island is one of the least known spots in the vicinity of New York. Having been for upwards of a century a military post, promiscuous visiting has not been encouraged and as a consequence few people are familiar with this beautiful Island, low lying just inside the gateway of our harbor.

The Island was ceded by the State of New York to the United States Government on condition that it be always kept as a military post. The exact date of this cession is somewhat clouded, but it was very early in the history of the republic, for there is a record of the building of a rally port and fort prior to 1800. This was named and is still called Fort Jay, after that patriotic American statesman who was the first chief justice of the supreme court of the United States.

Today the Island is used as headquarters for the Atlantic Division of the United States Army and of the Department of the East. In addition to the officers and their families, who live permanently there, it is occupied by four army companies and a military band, the total population averaging something like 400, exclusive of the military prisoners who are confined in Castle William, the old-fashioned round-tower fortress at the northwest corner of the Island. The number of these prisoners varies; at present there are about three hundred.

Strange as it may seem, this community with its captains and colonels and generals, its pretty villa houses, its many public buildings and barracks, lying almost within a stone's throw of the great metropolis of America in the Twentieth Century, up till a few months ago was compelled to rely for its artificial illumination entirely upon the old-fashioned kerosene lamp. When General Chaffee was in the Philippines he found the military posts there lighted by electricity. Upon his return the contrast between the archaic kerosene lighting of Governors Island and the up-to-date methods in the antipodes struck him as so different from what might reasonably be expected as to be actually ridiculous.

The results of an investigation then set on foot by the General was a contract made by the United States Government with the Brooklyn Edison Company to supply the Island. All of the buildings as well as the streets are now lighted by electricity.

South Street

"See the shaking funnels roar, with the Peter at the fore,
And the fenders grind and heave,
And the derricks clack and grate, as the tackle hooks the crate.
And the fall-rope whines through the sheave!"

—Where ships from all the seas come in!

Vagrant wind-jammers, from up and down the coast; high-sided whalers; tousled tramps, just in from 'round the Horn, lie side by side along the wharves. The aristocrats of the high-seas find their sleek sides under old and battered bowsprits.

Donkey-engines stutter and pant under cover of white-plumed steam-jets; hoarse voices call and answer in strange tongues; reef-points patter on taut-hung canvas, and a boatswain's whistle pipes shrill above the tumult!

There is an ineffable smell of tar and new paint; of sun-warmed varnish, and crusted sea-salt, hanging over these wanderers from many a distant harbour-bar, across ten thousand leagues of open sea.

Battery Park

While America may not yet be a nation of ruins, as some of her brethren across the water complain, still, the places which hold memories of her early history, are not among those which can easily be forgotten. Conspicuous, around the little park of Bowling Green, which may truly be called the cradle of the present tremendous city, is the "Custom House of the Port of New York," where three quarters of the duties of the country are collected; the United States Barge Office and the Aquarium.

In this ancient building, which echoed to the songs of Jenny Lind on her first appearance in America, may now be seen, some of the strangest and rarest denizens of the deep, gathered out of many seas.

From the vexed Bermudas, have been brought the parrot-fish, with its strange shape and startling col-

ors; from other waters, sea-cows and sea-elephants, trumpet-fish and splashing seals. The creatures of the deeps are laid before one, from giant, green-backed turtles to delicate, palpitating sea anemones, which close and fade at a passing shadow.

Fraunces Tavern

Since Nineteen hundred and four, nearly two hundred years after it had been built for the home of some of the great Dutch families, the Sons of the Revolution have shielded this relic of Colonial New York from the ruthless hand of progress.

In Seventeen hundred and sixty-two, it met what no doubt was then called its downfall, for swarthy Sam Fraunces, newly arrived from the West Indies, opened it under the Sign of Queen Charlotte, as "The Queen's Head Tavern."

Like many human catastrophies, this sliding downward in its social scale, finally raised the building to the pinnacle of fame and proved its passport through the ages, to stand, safeguarded and beloved, as long as one stone may rest upon another. There in the Long Room, on the second floor, the seeds of Liberty sprouted when the famous Stamp Act first heard itself speak, and there also, no doubt, the greatest of all " Tea Parties " and its bearings was discussed.

Early in December, Seventeen hundred and eighty-three a traveler on horseback splashed up the muddy street to the Tavern door. He had ordered dinner for " one hundred Generals, and Men of Distinction " who had given him eight years of most devoted and desperate service.

His name was George Washington, and the eloquence of his Farewell Address that evening to his Officers, left no one able to speak, and they parted in silence.

"—With a heart full of love and gratitude, I now take leave of you."

The toast of the evening, given for the first time in History was those five magic words which today cause nearly one hundred million hearts to throb wherever they may hear it, " The United States of America ! "

Curb Exchange

" Fifty-nine on a hundred gold! Fifty-nine on a ——"

" Taken! Close that up Jimmy—quick! "

And, waving at a window across the street, Jimmy lifts a hoarse cry above the tumult, while his fingers flash a few quick signals. The deal is closed! Five hundred shares have been sold " on the New York curb " and bought in the same manner and at almost the same time in Boston, three hundred miles away.

Every day, from ten to three, about two hundred yards of Broad Street is jammed with an excited multitude, buying and selling unlisted securities.

Over the office windows there are sign-boards, mounted with a row of electric bulbs, and under each of these, a number represents some salesman on the curb. Delays are so costly that the different firms have taken this positive method of signalling members of their staff.

Years ago, bids were written on sheets of paper and thrown down to the salesman from the office windows. But now, during a modern flurry, such a method becomes impossible, as the street is often lost in a chaos of waving arms and howling voices.

For this reason, the deaf and dumb alphabet has come to hold such complete sway that one may see a transaction involving thousands of dollars made and closed, simply on the crook of a finger.

J.P. MORGAN & C

Stock Exchange

Viewing the floor of the Stock Exchange from the visitors' gallery, it is sometimes difficult to imagine, that there must be method in the mad turmoil below. Some six or seven hundred men, are wildly waving, in a frenzy to make themselves heard.

"One thousand steel, one eighth!—five thousand, one fourth—!" Hats are knocked off; clothes disheveled, and still the strange calls and gestures continue, as white numbers appear and disappear on a huge blackboard. At times, the likeness of it all, to the antics of certain occupants in the zoo, becomes so striking as almost to arouse laughter.

Yet, when it is realized, that many of these same gestures, involve millions of dollars, a new respect is created for a body of men, whose integrity is so high, that dealings of such magnitude may be done on honor alone.

The privilege of doing business upon the floor of this building, which is a model one for its purpose, is valued at nearly one hundred thousand dollars.

In the lunch room upstairs, sometimes planning a new campaign with their brokers, while eating a frugal meal, may be seen those giants of the Exchange, whose operations in the market are of such magnitude as to make them always of interest to the whole financial world.

Wall Street

To many, Wall Street is but a name—and not one to conjure with at that. However, if one will but review its stirring history and people it, in imagination, with the figures of men who have loomed colossal in the annals of world-wide Finance, this short, narrow canyon, holds more of interest than perhaps any other street on the face of the globe.

Stand, for a moment, on the steps of the Sub-Treasury, and let the thrill and excitement of this, the richest and most powerful section of the world, creep into you, as the great loom of Wall Street stirs under its shuttle of hurrying messenger boys.

At every moment, fortunes are being made and lost, on this financial battleground, where all the panics that have rocked the nation, have been met and overcome.

Yet, it is but one hundred and twenty years since the historic figure of Washington stood here while he proclaimed the first establishment of our government.

The Sub-Treasury itself, holds one in amazement at the marvelous accuracy of hand and eye throughout all the intricate processes of counting and storing the coin of the realm. And outside, trucks filled with gold and silver ingots, arrive with so much unconcern, that one can hardly realize that this is the shimmering metal, for which men have fought and died since the Beginning of the Ages.

Singer Building

At different times in history treasures have been amassed, and always the methods of safeguarding them have been devious and intricate. But the days of the Pharaohs or Cæsars are not those of hurrying New York.

The modern treasure — almost beyond man's counting—is also placed far underground,—but in two steel vaults, which cost two hundred thousand dollars, and are today the strongest ever built!

The rusty key or secret counter-weight has been superseded by four electric timelocks, each acting independently of one another on the ponderous forty-thousand-pound doors,—for chance may not figure in guarding the entrance to where has lain five hundred million dollars!

Above these beautifully fitted vaults, is one of the most modern of office buildings. Its forty-eight electric elevators are in constant telephonic communication with the ground floor, besides having their position always indicated by means of an electric indicator-board placed in front of the "starter."

The unusual illumination of the tower at night, which has made it famous, is accomplished by twenty-nine eighteen-inch projectors, besides one of thirty inches, the duplicate of which is used at Sandy Hook, and is capable of throwing a beam of light up in the air to be visible for sixty miles.

The combined illumination from these projectors is estimated at the enormous figure of three and one-half million candle power.

World Building

Somebody once said that a city is only as good as its newspapers, and while this may be far from true, certainly no one will deny that an insight into the work of a great organization, which spends a million and a quarter dollars a year, gathering news, is inspiring to say the least.

From the dome, on a clear day, the horizon stretches away twenty miles distant, while in the near foreground stand some of the most beautiful and tremendous monuments of engineering skill ever erected. The Metropolitan Tower; the Brooklyn Bridge; the Singer Building; the East River Bridge; the Pennsylvania Terminal.

Throughout the fifteen stories below the dome, the whirl of life in a city of nearly five million inhabitants is being recorded, and the rushing, rumbling sound of it all makes the building seem like a thing alive.

Under the green-hued glare of the Cooper-Hewitt lights a great newspaper is forever in the throes of the latest edition,—printing one thousand tons of paper a week!

Two thousand people are at work—trying to do something just a little quicker than it was ever done before.

The smoking, pungent atmosphere of the photo-engraving rooms, is perpetually agleam with the fitful flicker of a fifty thousand candle power printing-lamp; incessant, the rattling clamor of fifty-six linotypes fills the long composing room, while far downstairs, ponderous electric presses,—the largest ever built,—scream and sob under the feverish pressure of nine hundred thousand copies an hour.

Everywhere, there is convulsive haste,—for the latest edition is going out!

Even the fierce light of modern science, can never pale the eternal miracle of the single slender wire, which leads the power five miles, to turn every cog in this throbbing activity where forty thousand pounds of molten metal are being shaped into the living stories of the day,—"tales of the bad, the sad, and the glad,—the regular quota of news"!

Post Office

The Post Office

Only a short span of one hundred years lies between the soap-box nailed to a tree, on the edge of the clearing, and the twenty million dollar Post Office, in the heart of the greatest metropolis of the Western Hemisphere.

But it is a far call, nevertheless, from the dusty, galloping pony-express, to the soughing, clanking gurgle of the electricity-driven pneumatic tubes that carry the mails deep under the city, to be finally distributed by an army of men, among the homes of the present generation.

More than one billion pieces of mail pass through this building every year, so that, even with the most up-to-date mechanical devices, a force of seven thousand people is needed to handle them with the quick accuracy which modern business methods demand.

Night and day, a legion of gray-coated men are patrolling the streets, making thirty-two separate collections and deliveries, from four thousand scattered letter-boxes.

A remarkable sight and one which can not be duplicated, even in this interesting branch of Uncle Sam's service, is that of sorting the mails. For hours at a time, men stand before serried rows of narrow pockets and with a deadly accuracy, born only of life-time practice, faster almost than the eye can follow, they flick letter after letter, sometimes to a distance of twenty feet, into the exact pouch, which is to take them on their final destination,—whether Persia or West Twenty-third Street.

The age of hand-canceled letters passed away forever when an electric "pick-up table" came into being. This novel machine will cancel both "longs" and "shorts" at the same time.

When in operation, the envelopes fly through it in two unbroken streams, — at the rate of seventy thousand an hour.

Seventy thousand letters an hour—what messages of Hope and Grief, of Love and black Despair, fluttering by, swifter even than the thoughts which wrote them.

Cherry Street Playground, underneath the Brooklyn Bridge

Decayed Gentility Cherry Hill

Ye Olde Tavern

Mayhap, since the days of seventeen hundred and ninety-seven, its solid oaken fittings with the copper nails, have acquired a darker tinge, and the row of pewter mugs a few more dents. But, call for a measure of musty ale, and it will be of the same quality which long ago caused men to stir in their sleep when the driver of the lurching stage called "Old Tavern,—First Stop!"

Dim, inviting corners, are tucked away in unexpected places and from some of these, occasionally, comes the soft rattle of shaken dice.

Overhead, racks of long-stemmed, church-warden pipes, corn tassels and bundles of flax, help to cast misshapen shadows round about. Once within its low-hung doors, and the busy murmur of the city dies away—the world steps back a hundred years.

Brooklyn Bridge

Hanging one hundred and thirty-five feet in the air from its stone piers, it swings out over the river in a single majestic arc,—this most famous suspension bridge in the world!

It is anchored at each end in a bed of thirty-five thousand cubic feet of solid masonry, and, since eighteen hundred and eighty-three, when it was finally completed at a cost of fifteen million dollars, its mile and one eighth of steel and stone has safely borne aloft the three hundred and fifteen thousand people who pass over it every day.

A network of transportation lines above and far below the river-bed, bind it fast to earth, seeming to give its gray aloofness a more human touch.

At night, from the raised promenade, may be seen the distant vagueness of the harbour, the great torch of the Statue of Liberty and the busy shipping on the river. And nearer, a fairy city, towered and turreted, stands pricked out in twinkling lights against the dark.

China Town

Very different it is now, from the days when Doyer Street was a black tunnel, which led off from the Bowery, behind a single dingy gas-jet. For, " them times we could see 'em comin' in—but they couldn't see *us!* "

True, the Joss-house is still there, under its garish, flaunting posters and Hop Wing's chicken chow-mien, with yuen sin chi, is just as good as it was ten years ago. But the plain-clothes squad, the tong feuds and the marvel of the incandescent bulb, have driven the old order of things to the wall. China-town is being scattered and some of its people are taking up new customs, though their hearts will never change. Always, they will be the same inscrutable, slant-eyed, shuffling men, who had an art and a religion that was old, three thousand years before America was born.

Yes, the old, true China-town has passed away! Woo Ling-soo claims that it went with the last of the Coolie-houses on Donivan's Lane—and Woo Ling-soo *knows,* for he still carries his queue hung down his back and is one of the only three men in the city today, who can tell of Donivan's Lane.

Donivan's Lane, of devious ways and many turnings; of hidden doors behind steep and crooked stairs,—the narrow rookerie-bordered path that once upon a time was known to open into Mott Street.

The Bowery

Men and boys, women and girls,—afloat, drifting to and fro, on the dark tide of the city's undertow. Every nation yields its flotsam, with the argot and the cant phrase from its streets. And under the hard lights, gape the ports of the derelicts,—pawn-shops, saloons and lodging-houses, dime theatres and more saloons.

The dreary, tuneless jangle from a dance hall is drowned for a moment in the thundering roar of a passing elevated, and from down the street comes the hollow boom of a Salvation Army drum.

And nearer, standing very still amid all the play of light and shadow, stretches the long line of those who have lost hold on the bottom rung. Some of them have stood there through five weary hours—waiting for a cup of coffee, and a bit of longed for bread. Hundreds of men, standing shoulder to shoulder in the great brotherhood of want!

MAX
EH

Push-Cart Town

The narrow, sunless streets, are filled with people from a thousand crowded homes. Everywhere, six and seven storied brick tenements are crowded to the eaves with humanity, for in this part of the town, one single square mile holds a quarter of a million people.

And the sights, and the sounds, and the strange odors, seem not to belong to hurrying New York, but to the outskirts of some of the most ancient cities in Europe.

Below the long line of smoking, flaring torches, Jews from every country under the sun, surge to and fro, laughing and gesticulating, as they bargain for everything from figs and bric-a-brac, to old lace and sheet-iron stove-tops. It is the market place of the Great East Side—the department store of the countless thousands, who know nothing of the city, five blocks from their own door.

Syrian Quarter
Lower West Side

An East Side Playground

A Recreation Pier Concert

East Side Street, Vendors

Little Hungary

Follow the sign of the big electric cross, turn into East Houston Street, and there in letters of fire is " Little Hungary."

Little Hungary, where more good wine sometimes seems to leak from the ceiling of the old cellar than materializes in the strange, uncanny bottles; where the very air is charged with gay frivolity and the brilliant Neapolitan singers are accompanied by the swirling, swinging cadence of the Hungarian orchestra.

It is here that the Ragged Edge Klub is known to meet, and it is also here, five years ago, that President Roosevelt held the banquet which he had promised in the days when he was Police Commissioner.

Laughter and jest and song ripple easily from table to table, while the air is heady with a strange aroma which is to be found nowhere else,—for this is the heart of Bohemia!

A Corner in the Syrian Quarter
Lower West Side

Francesca's

A quaint little Italian restaurant, replete with the atmosphere of the old Latin Quarter. There is, perhaps, not its like to be found anywhere in the City.

From the street, can be seen nothing more than a blue placard, bearing the legend " 64." Yet descend some worn stone steps, duck beneath a darkened, arching doorway, and one is on the sawdust strewn path that leads through the kitchen, out into a walled court-yard of the restaurant.

Round about, at intervals, are pictures, painted on the wall itself, by hands, some of which are long since dust. And in one corner a tree stands half imbedded in the masonry.

There is no orchestra; no carefully harmonized light effect and the radiators which do not radiate, stand out blatantly against the red brick wall. But then, where else may one have pink salad-dressing and the joy which comes of correctly deciding the great question of " Banan' or ze apple "?

Among its kind Francesca's stands unique. It's, well, it's,—just Francesca's.

Washington Arch

When a nation is very young, its history, while perhaps carrying great significance, does not always permit of many relics which bear tribute to past achievements.

Realizing this, the people of the United States of America caused to be erected, in eighteen hundred and eighty-nine, on the Centennial Anniversary of Washington's taking the oath of office, a marble arch which bears his name.

The exquisite design of its creamy white stone, for all its massive solidity, seems to idle in dreamy gentleness through long summer days against a green background of the park.

Thirty feet wide, it spans Fifth Avenue, and is arched just under the famous carved frieze, at a height of seventy-seven feet above the pavement.

It seems fitting that the one hundred and twenty-eight thousand dollars of its cost was borne by the people themselves, for on it are shaped the words which closed the inaugural address from the First President of the country.

"Let us raise a standard to which the wise and honest can repair. The event is in the hands of God."

SCHEFFEL

Scheffel-Halle

" Ich grüsse dich, du stolzes Haus,
Dich traute 'Scheffel-Halle'! "

It was in this old-time "Bierstube" that was forged a great part of the present strong chain of good-fellowship between American and German New York.

The fame of its true German dishes; its "Hasen-Pfeffer" stew with potato-balls; its rare old "Culmbacher" beer and Bretzels, has spread far indeed. For in that subtle atmosphere of "Gemüthlichkeit" there seems to be a friendly tinge on everything, from the iron scroll-work of the entrance to the stained-glass ceiling in the old hall itself.

When the ancient clock, up among the steins on the carved oaken mantel of the fire-place, slowly chimes that magic hour in which the spirit of the poet is supposed to stir abroad, the dim panels illustrating his many adventures, seem to gather up new life.

And then, just as they have done here every evening for more than thirty years, the four old German musicians will bend over their instruments for an "Abend-sang."

"— Fest steht, und treu die Wacht,—die Wacht am Rhein!"

Washington Irving's home
17th Street and Irving Place

Castle Cave

Under its smoke-darkened rafters, have been entertained many a famous person, for nowhere else in the city may one have delicacies, such as Mr. Bardusch himself broils beside the fragrant hickory-wood fire.

The shining meat-ax hangs against the wall, near the piled up hickory, and it catches the golden tints in the glow from the hot coals, when they are raked out and spread under the sizzling roasts.

By far, the most unique dish to be found in Castle Cave, is oysters on the half-shell, grilled, and brought, all steaming, to the table on a platter of live coals.

Metropolitan Tower

The long, swift rise of an electric express elevator—forty-four stories without a stop; two turns in a narrow stairway, and one is out on the balcony of the second tallest structure in the world. Within sight lie the homes of one sixteenth of all the people in the United States.

Here, one may toss a penny nearly seven hundred feet sheer, down into a pigmy city which has dropped so far away that, but for a distant murmur, it seems to carry on its work in perpetual silence.

Vast, nebulous, smoke-hung New York,—the land that Peter Minuit once bought for twenty-four dollars' worth of trinkets! Somewhere, of course, steam riveters are thundering as they fling up new sky-scrapers; fire-gongs are ringing and whistles blowing; crimes and brave deeds are being heralded. But no sound of it save that steady undertone of traffic ever reaches up beyond the sun-gilded banners of steam, for at this height even the whimpering winds seem to pause for a moment as if in doubt.

Perhaps the most interesting thing about the tower is the tremendous, electric four-dial clock. It is the largest that has yet been built, with a minute hand seventeen feet long and weighing half a ton.

Strange, indeed, it seems, to hear the old, historic Cambridge chimes, ring out on the quarter hours at a height of nearly fifty floors above the sidewalk, and to know that two-hundred-pound elec-

tric hammers are striking them on seven-thousand pound bells.

Within the building,—a small city in itself—five thousand people are at work keeping the records of the biggest life insurance business ever developed.

The walls are made of pure Tuckahoe marble and exquisitely chased bronze. And it took sixteen years before they were finally in place,—on this compeer of the distant Tomb of Agra by the broad white road to Delhi.

Overlooking Madison Square Park

Its duplicate is not to be found anywhere, for it is the only hotel of its kind in the world.

This original project was financed by the Women's Hotel Corporation, which designed and erected it exclusively for women. There are women clerks and girl " bell-boys."

No matter how unprotected a young girl may be who comes alone to town, with " Martha Washington " for a chaperon, she is considered as safe as in her own home. Not even brothers or fathers may stay over-night within its sacred portals or penetrate above the parlor floor.

The four hundred and fifty rooms, accommodate six or seven hundred guests, and on the top of its twelve stories, there is a fine roof-garden.

Situated, as the Martha Washington is, in the very center of interesting activities, from its doorway one might shoot an arrow into several of the big women's camps without stirring.

The Women's University Club with a membership list of seven hundred lies close by, and slightly farther away, the head-quarters of the Women's Suffrage movement which is now over sixty thousand strong; the Colony Club; the Women's Municipal League and the exhibit of the Consumer's League which demonstrates by means of models and photographs, the evils which arise from sweat-shop work among the tenements.

Madison Square Garden from the Park

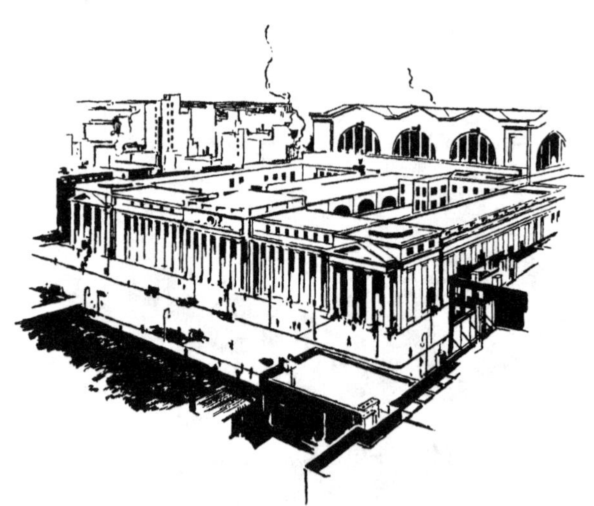

He stands looking gravely down on the people who hurry by,—the people who are too busy even to gaze about them on the work to which he gave his life. A slender bronze statue of Alexander Cassat, holding an open book within one hand. His was the vision and the force necessary to carry this gigantic project through to its present conclusion.

It was a long fight and a hard one, but he never wavered. Insurmountable difficulties arose; traffic and organization problems presented themselves that had never even been heard of before, and he conquered them all—though at what cost to himself no one will ever know!

In due time he extended the railroad, of which he was president, to nine acres of valuable land in the heart of New York City. He accomplished the ideal for which he had dreamed and striven,—and the price of the accomplishment, was one hundred and fifty million dollars!

But far greater than this is the fact that the visible result, with its vaulted arches and sweet-sounding echoes, is a thing of stately beauty from the genius of McKim, Meade and White, and one of which the city may always well be proud.

A Great Retail Business

It is very hard, when stepping into this modern colossus of the selling world, to realize the years of patient, plodding toil which lie beneath it,—the hopes and dreams of men who have been planning this ideal of theirs for more than a generation.

Away back in the early forties, when transportation was by wagon and French money was used west of the Ohio, Adam Gimbel was already a leading merchant in the little town of Vincennes, Indiana.

Here, beneath the flaring lanterns in his small two story "Trade Palace," he exchanged, among other things, plug tobacco and calico for pelts.

And this is a far cry from the most modern of great retail stores with its twenty-seven acres of space, its six thousand employes, its six million dollar building, its thirty-six elevators, one thousand telephones, and miles upon miles of electric wiring. Yet, throughout all this, there runs a pleasing thread of simplicity,—the stately simplicity of solid mahogany, white marble, and perfect arrangement.

Figures carry little meaning when they compass such quantities as are beyond human experience, but it can be readily seen how the tremendous vastness of such an enterprise would be overpowering were it not for clever architectural handling of space. In this regard the Tea Room stands preeminent. Here, the entire population of some New England towns might be seated and be far from crowded. Still, in some miraculous manner, the impression of quiet cosiness remains.

It is very safe to say that Gimbel's is the last whisper in the evolution of the science of selling. Rest rooms; silence rooms; a fully equipped hospital with a physician and nurse in charge; a luxurious waiting room; concerts of grand opera; all these and more, show the fullest realization of the policy of making the customer comfortable.

But greater than all this material growth is the stupendous fact that Gimbel's was the first store to advertise that its social conscience had awakened. Before it opened, there appeared in huge letters, with its other advertisements on the outside of the building, the pregnant words,

"We will not carry either Child Labor or Sweat-shop goods! Everything will be Economically as well as Physically clean!"

Rector's

And who has not heard of Rector's!

The salle-a-manger in this Aladdin's palace of crimson and marble and gold has the name of being among the most beautiful rooms ever designed.

Rare mosaics of stained glass, paintings and marbles, sometimes half-hidden behind green palms, all lend a subtle, unobtrusive splendor. While two great chandeliers hanging near either end, and made from thousands of tiny pieces of hand-cut, rosy-tinted glass, are forever glowing, a-quiver with whimsical lights.

But it is more interesting to see the place from whence emerges that miraculous Filet of Sea-bass and the Vol-au-vent which has made this restaurant famous across two continents.

It presents, with its equipment of every known implement, a remarkable scene of well-ordered, adroit activity; comparable only to the decks of a warship before going into action. For the first time in history, French art has been combined with American silent speed and efficiency.

And the result? Ah!—cela se laisse manger!

Canfield's Bronze Door

The evening, four years ago, when Commissioner Jerome swung his ax,—and broke it,—on the famous twenty-eight thousand dollar bronze door of Canfield's gambling house, was a memorable one in the police annals of the city. The marks are there yet,—only two tiny gashes—for the hardened metal, which, in fifteen hundred and thirty, used to guard the wine-cellar of a great palace, is some four inches thick.

What strange scenes, through all the passing years, must the playful cherubs, which decorate its massive front, have looked upon! Yet, now that the place has become a restaurant, they behold nothing more startling than a throng of city-dwellers, bent on taking dinner upstairs, where the tables are set under the most expensive ceiling in New York.

The famous mahogany railing on the stair-case is upheld by many dancing nymphs, each of which was carved in different form from a solid block at an enormous cost.

Downstairs, drinks are now served in the same room where, formerly, the chips were bought or cashed in, and where it is rumored a well-known millionaire, one evening, left one hundred and fifty thousand dollars.

"And Now Let Us Conserve Human Life"

The great bound with which the question of "Social Insurance" sprang into prominence of late, has brought the American Museum of Safety within the spot-light of public interest.

This exhibit, includes protecting devices for the safeguarding of human life, in almost every field of labor, from the turning of a grindstone to the moving of a freight train,—yet, unusual and interesting as it is now, bewildering, in an array of strange appliances, it gives but a conception of how far this new movement may some day be carried.

On one side, the demonstrator is explaining the use of a valve-lock which prevents a man who is cleaning the inside of a boiler, from being grilled alive by someone carelessly turning on the steam. Passing on, he picks a can of gasoline from a rack and setting fire to it, calmly pours a flaming stream from one container to another, in proof of his statement that this high explosive is now no more dangerous than water,—when protected with a small device.

Safety-exits, which open automatically on contact with a person's body; devices for protecting punches and presses; safety-scaffolding; and protection for life at sea; respirators, for use in mine disasters; together with innumerable machines, models and photographs, form a collection of intense interest even to the ordinary observer and of incalculable value to manufacturers in general. For at present, annually in the United States, over five hundred thousand men are being wiped out from the ranks of the wage-earners,—a loss to the cash wealth in the country of two hundred and fifty million a year!

And so it is, that this museum is fast becoming the protecting bulwark at the top of America's industrial precipice. It is heading the momentous change which is sweeping so rapidly over the country at large—the change from inadequate and costly Compensation to the cheaper and more humane Prevention.

Residence of J. P. Morgan
36th Street and Madison Avenue

Murray's

A myriad many-colored lights; glowing, reflected again and yet again, deep-set in a sea of mirrors; the soft splash of a tumbling fountain which bursts from beneath the feet of a marble goddess; the subdued hum of soft laughter mingled with the tinkle of silver and crystal and under all the voice of the singing, wailing violins—this is Murray's!

Entering the "Roman Garden" directly from the street we are translated, as if by Mahomet's carpet, from the prosaic influence of Times Square to the luxurious, indolent atmosphere of Rome at the zenith of the Cæsars.

The scheme of decoration produces an outdoor effect, which is heightened by a blue sky, twinkling with electric stars, and overswept by moving artificial clouds.

Around the rooms, behind columned panels, have been painted views in keeping with the style of decoration and which lend an enchanting sense of perspective to the scene. Many of these are of the renowned White collection and go far towards upholding that remarkably artistic *tout ensemble*, which, from the entrance to the roof-garden, has made Murray's famous as far as the Pacific Slope.

Sherry's

Every name carries with it some association.

Sherry's, to the New Yorker, has long, among other things, meant especially that place where the fashionable bride-to-be may entertain her friends, either at dinner or in the afternoon over a cup of tea, while continually past the spacious windows, flows the ever-changing kaleidoscope of the Avenue.

Here, in the evening, under the soft lights, may be seen many fair women and noted men, for from farewell bachelor suppers of the Smart Set, to the exclusive Patriarch Ball, many different noteworthy entertainments have given Sherry's the reputation it now bears of being, perhaps more than any other place, the favorite resort of the *elite*.

Delmonico's

When "Delmonico and Brothers" opened a coffee, cake and confectionery shop in the year eighteen hundred and twenty-eight at Number Twenty-three William Street, "they and the female members of their family dispensed coffee, liquor, pâtés and confections." Undoubtedly, they little dreamed of such an organization as was later to spring from this single small room.

When, in eighteen hundred and forty-two John Delmonico, then the head of the house, passed away, his family had printed in a local paper this unique notice, so filled with the atmosphere of seventy years ago.

"A CARD: The widow, brother and nephew Lorenzo of the late much respected John Delmonico tender their heartfelt thanks to the friends, benevolent societies and Northern Liberty Fire Engine Company, who accompanied his remains to his last home. The establishment will be re-opened to-day, under the same firm of Delmonico Brothers, and no pains of the bereft family will be spared to give general satisfaction. Restaurant, bar-room, and private dinners, Number Two South William Street; furnished rooms Number Seventy-six Broad Street, as usual."

And so it has,—but evidently always a little *better* than "usual"! For from "dispensing bonbons, coffee and liquor" it has risen gradually to be "Delmonico's"—the most famous restaurant in existence to-day!

Ritz-Carlton

While it could hardly be said that the phrase "one finds one's warmest welcome at the inn" would ever apply to any part of such a tremendous organization as the Ritz-Carlton hotel-chain, yet strangely enough, for all its modernity, this very feeling has been here in part preserved.

True, the superb appointments of the halls and dining rooms, with their artistic reflected-lighting effects, conjure up very different visions from the gooseberry pie and rare roast beef which made famous the inns of Hawthorne's and Dickens' time.

There are travelers who know fine hotels the world over and yet will stay in none which does not bear the crest of the Ritz-Carlton, whether they happen to be in New York or London, Madrid or St. Petersburg.

Plaza

The Plaza

The Merchant Princes of mediæval Venice, with their open-handed patronage of art, could hardly boast of higher attainments in interior architecture, than the modern hotel-palaces for which New York is noted.

Like Ashley House in London and the Madeleine in Paris, the Plaza is in possession of a situation which will never retrograde, no matter where following decades may carry the city's limits, for it stands at the barrier of Central Park,—the broad expanse of green trees and sparkling lakes which stretches three miles Northward from its door.

It is hard to conceive of an hotel, so immense as to require a complete silversmith, upholstery plant and corps of mattress makers within its walls.

Yet for all its sixteen million dollar building and countless servants, the Plaza has always retained that indescribable something which brings its guests back year after year.

Perhaps it is the sheer physical beauty of its fittings as in the famous tea room, with its Patio-like spaces and dome of softly tinted glass; its columnade of Fleur de Peche marble and golden-bronze columns. Or then, again, it may be the charm of the music on the terrace-gardens—such music as may be only purchased for the sum of sixty thousand dollars a year!

But whatever the reason, nothing can dim the fact that the Plaza has rightly earned for itself the name of a wonderful and magnificent hotel.

Central Park

The March to Victory is ever an entrancing subject, but perhaps never more so than in St. Gaudens' masterpiece, under the shadows of which one steps within the magic eight hundred and forty acres of Central Park.

It is at its best early on a spring morning,—so early as to create the feeling that it belongs with all its freshness to one human alone. Then, the sheep are out with their little lambs; the squirrels seem more tame, and gaze in friendly fashion; while the white swans in their stately splendor have already established title to the lakes. Myriad sweet-voiced birds hold council up in the foliage, for this is the chosen resting place of winged wanderers as they pursue their way North and South within the year.

Many of the trees have been brought from under foreign skies, to be planted here by distinguished visitors.

But when Cleopatra made her needles, four thousand years ago, she little thought that one would be taken from the Temple of the Sun, lost at sea, and found again, to stand at the Temple of Art in a New World, where soon, among its other treasures, it is hoped to find Rembrandt's half-million dollar Mill.

All through the Park, sometimes half-hidden amidst the trees, stand guardian statues of those patriots who have served the republic well, while at night the Harlem Meer recalls King Arthur's legends, quivering light-reflections in the lakes, dream-palaces of old.

Up in the telegraph room at headquarters, an officer's terse report is coming in over the telephone to be put on record,—though it is but seven minutes since the first gong was struck,—"Ten-sixty-five, First Avenue, — Sub-basement, — Two Companies" and that is all! A man holds his finger on a chart for a moment while he makes a few notations and the quick scratching of his pen is distinctly audible in the uncertain pause, before the swift, steady menace of the alarm breaks in again.

Headquarters has been known to receive more than one hundred and fifty calls in one day, which is a higher number—except for some great disaster—than has been rung up in any other fire department ever organized.

It is known that New York City spends seven and one half million dollars every year putting out thirteen thousand fires, but much of this undoubtedly is paid for being ready to put out untold more, which possibly might have occurred. And it is just this point of being ready, which has contributed perhaps more than anything else to making the New York Fire Department, with its one hundred and sixty engines, sixty-five hook and ladder companies, seven fire boats, and training school, what it is to-day—the most efficient on the globe.

The American Museum of Natural History

What the "Zoo" is to the Londoner, this Museum of Natural History is to the dweller in New York. He may well be proud, for in its possession are many specimens which can be seen nowhere else.

Neither expense nor trouble is spared in sending expeditions of scientific men to all quarters of the globe, to study, and collect new specimens; while citizens of the republic also donate objects which they acquire in every country. So it happens, that, among other interesting things, one finds here, Peary's sledge which reached the Pole; the animals Roosevelt shot at the equator; the Tiffany collection of gems; Meteorites fallen from among the stars to be found and brought home out of the Northland; butterflies, so beautiful as to almost make one believe they were captured by a magic net in Fairyland, and that miraculous substance called Radium, whose powers are not yet even understood.

Primitive peoples, from almost all climes and all ages, are resuscitated in their natural surroundings. The prehistoric and those who have perished since their contact with civilization,—Aztecs and Cliff-Dwellers; Incas from Peru, and Cannibals from the Land of Fire.

But it is the skeleton of the Dinosaur, hanging in the main hall, which is always the center of interest. Being the only one in existence, men have traveled some ten thousand miles merely to gaze upon the figure of this monster creature, which ruled upon earth ten millions of years ago.

MYERS
NY 1911
Mall Concert Central Park NY

The Speedway. Washington Heights

Soldiers' and Sailors' Monument
Riverside Drive

Riverside Drive

Riverside Drive

What La Cornichi is to the old world, Riverside is to the new.

But the beauties of Riverside are not easy things to see, for across the Hudson lie the Palisades,—the Palisades that will never grow old, while sunlight and shadow play their many fancies among the castled battlements and towers.

The individual character of the drive is hardly paralleled by any of the world's most famous avenues, for even though it is faced with some of the handsomest residences in America, still, at many places the woods have been left undisturbed in their native charm.

A temple, sometime to be the greatest ever built, stands close upon its path, and nearby is Columbia College which in seventeen hundred and sixty-four was granted to " The City of New York in America " by King George the Third.

Two tombs, and only two, are given honor upon this parkway. They stand near together upon the bluff, and each, with a touch of noble dignity, carries its separate message to the world.

Upon the first, which has stood here more than a hundred years, there reads the simple words " To an amiable child—aged five."

And on the second, the words of him who, when still in the flush of a victory, which had welded fifty million people, could only say,

" Let us have peace! "

College of the City of New York

St. John The Divine
on
Cathedral Heights

Churches of New York

Despite America's reputation for commercialism, her principal city might almost be called a City of Churches,—a town where it is easily possible for one to attend both morning and afternoon services every day for a year and yet never set foot twice in the same building!

About fifty years after the advent of the Pilgrims, Old Trinity was built. It stands at the head of Wall Street on what is undoubtedly the most valuable piece of Church land in the world, and many a time have its sweet bells rung out the old and in the new-born year.

Further up town, Grace Church, with its open-air pulpit, its lawns and shrubbery and its atmosphere of peaceful quiet, suggests somehow, even in the roar of the traffic along Broadway, the placid tranquillity of old England.

But the list might be extended almost without end, from the enormous St. Patrick's which in purity of style and beauty of material is hardly surpassed by any in the world, down to the "Little Church Around the Corner," with its vine covered walls, its lych-gate and drinking fountain.

Many churches, stately and beautiful, has New York. But it is this Little Church Around the Corner which perhaps lies nearest of all to the hearts of the people, for ever since it came into existence, it has been the refuge of the stricken and the wearied, the homeless and oppressed.

"Little Church Around the Corner"
29th Street and Fifth Avenue

Bronx Park

"—Where winds the Bronx!" for what other cities have a river, which rises, flows and empties, within their gates?

Upon the four thousand acres of this great breathing space of New York, where is intended room for all the millions still to come within her borders, one may do many things.

There is a river to row upon; a magnificent golf course; the Sound to swim in; woods to walk among; or the Botanical and Zoological Gardens to visit.

And eons ago a rocking-boulder of some thirty tons, was left in this natural park to be a plaything of Man when the Great-Ice departed.

RESTAURANT

Coney Island

" Come!—*see-e* the big show—big show! *Only* five cents!—*half* a dime!—the twentieth part of a dollar! Step *right* up!—men, women *and* little children! *See-e* dreadful Emo, the Turtle-Boy! Writhing, twisting, turning, all the times!—*Captured in the wilds of Africa!*

What childhood memories does not the place recall, with its indescribable sound of blaring bands and booming drums; shrill-voiced venders and shouting " barkers " over the steady murmur of laughing crowds.

" Soda! Cider! Sas'parilla — *all* y' wan'er drink fer fi-ive cents! "

A wheezy, gurgling hand-organ is trying to make itself heard, while the monkey in its little red jacket and bells, crouches half-defiantly upon its perch. From a-far off comes the shrieking joy of children on the shute-the-shutes and the smell of new-made candy is everywhere.

Above is the warm sky and time seems made to spend with lavish hand, for the same old spirit of adventure is in the air, which used to thrill at circus time!

Navy Yard

When Universal peace shall come to rule, undoubtedly this birthplace of olden time "Ships of the Line," shall pass away. But always by the Wallabout there will remain the marble censer from the hand of Macmonnies, for it symbolizes the resting place of those who perished on the *Jersey*—the prison-hulk of the Revolution.

At present, in the Basin, lie sturdy transports; slender, venomous "destroyers"; submarines and torpedo-boats—the fighting machines that guard a nation's honor.

Trophies of the prowess of the Navy are everywhere. Among them, mortars and captured guns; fragments of shells and historical curiosities.

But it is the old wooden frigate *Vermont*, which seems to embody the atmosphere of departed conflict. Its great yellow bulk is housed over, and moored for the last time; its fighting days gone by,—for it has seen the game played out. Once, it shook under the thunder of smoking guns while its decks ran slippery with blood. Yet now, still faithful, it serves with the rest of this station as a place where men may live in peace and learn the art of war.

Looking Across the River

A Trip Up the Hudson

Why America listens with complacency when her Hudson is called the American Rhine, is hard to understand. For, from the great city by the bay, "singing like a forest of stone in the breath of the Atlantic," far up to the Old Crow's Nest, near which Washington Irving has thrown a mystic thrall, it needs no Lorelei to enhance its ever-changing charms.

The same sheer Palisades, at which Hudson marveled from his tiny "Half-Moon," as he pushed sturdily Northward towards the goal of his ambition, are there today; Indian Head still looks down upon the river; Storm King beckons to the thunder clouds, as they did in sixteen nine.

"Its morning and evening reaches are like the still lakes of a dream! Yet no river is so lordly in its bearing—none flows in such state to the sea"!

One used to be told that all good Americans were to visit Paris *when* they died. But now it has come to pass that all good golfers are promised a visit to New York *before* they die!

In all directions, lie some of the most noted links of the country. The nearest, perhaps, is in Van Cortlandt Park, which is so accessible as easily to permit of a round before dinner. Slightly farther out of town lies the Montclair Golf Club, having in addition to its fine course, perhaps, the most remarkable view of anywhere about.

Mention might be made of the Oakland, on Long Island, with its hills and almost impossible gullies; the easier and more beautiful Briarcliff overlooking the Hudson, and the Garden City Link,—that "maker of experts,"—near which Travis and Alexander Smith have their homes.

Then too, not to be forgotten, is the Nassau Golf Club at Glen Cove with its springy turf and velvety greens; the up-and-down concealed-hole course at Fox Hills on Staten Island, where is found the dreadful "Hell's Kitchen"; and on the slope of the Orange Mountains the Baltusrol of Short Hills, New Jersey, a difficult, sporty course where from a beautiful club-house may be had a fine outlook upon the surrounding country.

There is also the Apawanis, a long, narrow and difficult eighteen-hole course, which is known to try severely the caliber of any amateur.

But he who can run up even the most miserable score upon the famous National of Long Island, may consider himself skilled indeed. Neither time, trouble nor expense has been spared in making this the hardest, as well as the most original course, to be found anywhere. For here, in every green, is found an exact copy of the difficult hole in each of the eighteen remarkable courses of Europe.

The New York High Pressure Water System

There is probably no more impressive sight in the every-day life of New York than that of one of its monster glittering fire-fighters dashing along an avenue drawn by a trio of handsome plunging horses, belching forth smoke and leaving in its wake a glowing trail of embers, while all traffic halts and flat-dwellers rush to their windows.

This picturesque method of fire-fighting is now becoming extinct and in its place is the modern efficient high-pressure system: in fact it is the present purpose of the Fire Department eventually to discard all portable pumping engines and to rely entirely upon high pressure.

The power necessary to drive these pumps of

heretofore unheard of capacity is electrical and is supplied by The New York Edison Company at 6,600 volts from Waterside Station.

The high pressure zone on Manhattan Island is bounded by the Hudson River on the West; Twenty-third Street on the North; Broadway to Fourteenth Street, Fourth Avenue and Bowery on the East; and Chambers Street on the South. There are two pumping stations, one located near the Gansevoort Market on the North River, the other on the corner of Oliver and South Streets, near the East River, both being outside of the district of high risk which they were built to protect.

Both of the pumping stations have a capacity of 15,000 gallons per minute, aggregating for both 43,000,000 gallons per day. This amount is equal to two-thirds of the total quantity of fresh water used by the Borough of Manhattan for fire extinguishing purposes during the year 1903. Each station contains five pumping units, consisting of Allis-Chalmers multi-stage, centrifugal pumps, each driven by an Allis-Chalmers eight-hundred-horse-power induction motor.

All of the pumps are capable of delivering 3,000 gallons per minute, against a discharge pressure of 300 pounds per square inch when operating at 750 revolutions per minute. The controllers and motors are so designed that they can be brought up from a standstill to full speed in approximately thirty seconds, while the high-pressure system will reach 300 pounds pressure within one minute from starting the pumps.

There are high-pressure hydrants within 400 feet of any building in the danger zone, and there are enough hydrants so that sixty streams of 500 gallons per minute can be concentrated on a block, with a length of hose not exceeding 400 to 500 feet.

It is easy to comprehend what a dreadful disaster would result were this high-pressure system to be suspended for any period of time when seriously needed. In order to offset the possibility of such a catastrophe The New York Edison Company has taken every precaution known to science and skill to fortify its service against trouble, while in its contract with the city it agrees to forfeit $500.00 per minute for any interruption of its service of over three minutes at the pumping stations.

The Great White Way. Twenty-five Electric Signs are Shown in this Picture

Broadway at Night

If, at any time since the beginning of history, Commerce has been touched with the magic wand of Romance, it is when " Broadway is a-blaze under the stars."

Far reaching, intricate campaigns of publicity are now mapped out and executed, by high-salaried specialists, in much the same manner that generals lay their plans before manœuvering into battle.

Every penny of the appropriations, some of which often soar near the million mark, is spent only with full knowledge of the exact effect it will have upon the public mind,—and pocket book. It presents the last and most fascinating aspect of psychology carried to its fullest development.

Literally, some ten years ago, night was completely driven from a large section of Broadway,—probably never to return.

The New Custom House

The changeful lights throw a glamour over the faces in the hurrying crowds,—the crowds that the men, who are spending fortunes in advertising, are trying to reach. Faces in joy, in sorrow and in pain; and faces that Death has traced his finger upon, for here there is every type of civilization—the Froth and the Dregs rub elbows.

Over all, a perpetual brilliance reigns, for no sooner do the first shadows of evening attempt to recapture their own, than countless electric signs, of every hue and description, spring into being.

A huge eagle, with a fluttering ribbon caught in his beak, begins to flap on his nightly journey towards a five-foot bottle of beer; a kitten, to tangle and untangle herself in a spool of well-known silk. And soon, far skyward, down the dazzling thoroughfare, a chariot race begins,—the Great White Way is a-stir again!

Central Park, Looking toward Columbus Circle

The Edison Electric Illuminating Company of Brooklyn

Brooklyn, the descendant of the old Dutch burgh of Breukelen, with its quaint Dutch traditions and multitude of churches and homes, is the home of one of the five largest lighting companies in the country, The Brooklyn Edison Company. Since it was organized in 1888 the population it supplies has increased from 600,000 to 1,700,000, and all the while the Company has developed and extended in even greater proportion.

The Brooklyn Edison Company supplies a fan-shaped territory seventy-seven square miles in area. At the apex of the imaginary fan is Brooklyn Bridge and at its zenith is Coney Island. On January 1st, 1890, the Company's load was 6,600 fifty-watt equivalents and on January 1st, 1911, 2,050,000 fifty-watt equivalents, the capacity of its two generating stations being 50,000 kilowatts. The business runs along the usual lines, except that The Brooklyn Edison Company has been more fortunate than others in having been able to develop a tremendous load at Coney Island which fills in the Summer "valley," so that the July and December peaks are nearly the same, a condition which exists in probably no other central station.

Thus it happens that the annual peak does not occur in the two or three weeks prior to Christmas, but in September, when the great Coney Island Mardi Gras trade and the load due to the beginning of the city season cross. This peak is still higher than the Christmas holiday peak. Coney Island has the most massive show of decorative lighting of any amusement resort in the world. It is the original example of the use of light as the chief attraction and has been imitated the world over, bringing business to thousands of central stations throughout the country.

The Brooklyn Edison Company under the leadership of its president, Mr. Anthony N. Brady, has gained prominence in the electric lighting fraternity of late for its pioneer work in the employee profit-sharing scheme. It was also one of the first companies to take up the company section work for the National Electric Light Association, and has been active in that organization for a number of years.

Madison Square Park. The Flatiron and Fifth Avenue Buildings

Central Park

New York and Queens Electric Light and Power Company

A tract of land a mile wide and extending from City Hall, New York, to the steps of the Capitol at Albany is an area equal to that served by The New York and Queens Electric Light and Power Company. In this Company's territory could be placed Manhattan, Brooklyn and half of the Bronx. It extends from the East River to Jamaica Bay and from the Brooklyn boundary to Long Island Sound.

This great area was once composed of numberless little independent municipalities, which in 1897 were consolidated and became a part of Greater New York. The existing lighting company was organized in 1900 and represents a consolidation of more than a dozen smaller companies.

The district is one of the most cosmopolitan anywhere outside of the metropolis itself. Within it are the magnificent residences of the very wealthy, the modest homes of the middle class, and the humble dwellings of the very poor. There are the great factories where thousands are employed, as well as small factories of every description. The power and street lighting loads are the largest. On the latter is one of the biggest systems of series incandescent street lighting in the country.

Owing to the vastness of the territory covered by this lighting company there is necessarily a tremendous investment in cable, poles, wires, etc. During the year 1910 there were erected 2,200 new poles, 82 tons or 1,500,000 feet of copper wires were strung, and 150,000 feet of cable were laid. All of this was simply additional to the existing installation at that time, the total capacity of the generating station being 7,500 kilowatts.

City Hall Park. The World Dome in the Background

Flatbush Gas Company

Back in the good old days, now hardly to be conceived from the rapid changes making us alive with wonderment, when the old town of Flatbush was quite isolated from Breukelen, the inhabitants thought well of the old tallow dip made by the thrifty housewife, and only with some misgiving passed on from this primitive method to the more practical kerosene oil lamp. This was indeed an awakening, but a still bolder step was taken in 1864 when such prominent representatives of the community as John A. Lott, John Lefferts, John J. Vanderbilt, Henry Wall, Homer L. Bartlett and Abraham Lott formed The Flatbush Gas Company.

These gentlemen saw that progression was leading them to the time when to be without their own gas, electric and water plants meant that they were not giving their children the benefits of enhanced values of real estate by the introduction of such commodities, and so they acted. Previous to 1894 The Flatbush Gas Company manufactured nothing but gas, but in that year an electric generating station was built. For a long time the current was used only for street lighting, but in the last ten years residential lighting has had a continuous growth due mainly to the large number of fine types of homes that have been erected in this exclusive section. The capacity of the generating station is rated at 4,500 kilowatts.

In 1636 a sturdy little band of voyagers imbued with the traditions of Old Holland, their mother country, selected "Midwout," now Flatbush, as the ideal place for their homes on the new continent. Midwout was the most central of the "Five Dutch Towns" and was early made the county seat of Kings County. The spirit of the early settlers still proves true of the enterprising men and women of today who live amid the attractive environments of Flatbush and its stimulating force is felt in the varied social and religious activities of the one-time Dutch Village.

Queens Borough Gas and Electric Company

A territory eighteen miles long by about a mile and a half wide, a large part of which was sand dunes and marsh lands less than twenty-five years ago, is that served by the Queens Borough Gas and Electric Company of Far Rockaway. Part of this is the beach property of the Rockaways, where a great Summer business is done, while the Long Island towns in the western part of Nassau County are included in the area.

Twenty-five years ago Rockaway Beach was unheard of, except as a fishing or clam digging place, and the towns on the adjacent mainland were not known to fame. In those days, the "natives" reached the city only after a tedious journey by stage to the town of Jamaica, where they boarded the trains of the Long Island Railroad. With the extention of the railroad lines to the beaches, began

Herald Square. Herald Building on the Right

the boom of the resorts, and now they rank with the most popular of New York's watering places.

Electricity was first used in the late eighties, with hardly enough customers to pay the expenses of the generating plant. In the Summer of 1910 there were in use 3,070 meters, more than double those in use at the same season five years ago. The generating plant of the Company is at Far Rockaway, with sub-stations at Rockaway Park and Lynbrook. Its equipment consists of two 300 kilowatt generators, one 600, one 1,500 and a 2,500 kilowatt generator which has just been installed to meet this year's demand. There are eighty-five miles of pole line. On the beach properties where it has been necessary to use oil barrels, the poles are set in the sand. More than seventy-five percent of the gas mains are laid below the high water mark.

Richmond Light and Railroad Company

The Richmond Light and Railroad Company, established in August, 1902, is the result of a combination of two other companies, the Staten Island Lighting Company and the Staten Island Railroad Company, the former of which in its day was a union of two or three smaller concerns.

This Company has from the start furnished current for the whole Island, or a territory of seventy-five square miles with a population of 85,000. Much of the country is rural, comprising miles of unsettled farm land.

Use of electricity, however, is pretty general, many of the farm houses even being connected. There is one instance of an entire dairy being operated by electricity, with electric milkers, separators, and so forth. All the ship yards with one exception, and nearly all the factories, together with the ferry and municipal buildings, are supplied by the Richmond Light and Railroad Company.

During the last five years there has been an increase in the lighting of 300%. Practically every new house is wired for electricity. The railroad end of the business, comprising thirty-one miles of road, shows a slight increase; and although a steam road runs on a parallel line, the electrics get their share of the trade. In Summer there is enough travel to keep both exceedingly busy. This Company operates in addition the Midland Railroad with a mileage of 29.

The total power generated for both light and railroad during the past year was 13,658,769 kilowatts. The Summer load is carried for South Beach and a portion for Midland which has a small plant of its own.

The United Electric Light and Power Company

The United Electric Light and Power Company was the first electric lighting company to extend its service north of Fifty-ninth street and at present is the only one serving the territory north of 135th street. This Company supplies alternating current exclusively within the Borough of Manhattan from its underground mains widely distributed from the Battery to the Harlem Ship Canal. The service is of a frequency of 60 cycles, single phase and two-phase in character.

The three-phase, 7500 volt generating apparatus is located at Waterside Stations No. 1 and No. 2 and transmitted over three-conductor 250,000 c. m. cables to the two sub-stations, where transformation is made from three-phase to two-phase, three-wire, and to the distributing voltage of 2100 volts across each phase (3000 volts across the outer conductors).

The sub-stations are located at 208–210 Elizabeth street, covering the lower section of the city, and at 519 West 146th street, supplying the central and upper sections. These two sub-stations are similar in most respects except as to capacity. Transformation is by air blast, transformer sets, and motor generators.

The general offices are located at 1170 Broadway, with branch offices and display rooms at 138 Hamilton Place, near 143rd street. The maximum load of the Company is in excess of 12,000 kilowatts, with a connected load of 940,000 50-watt equivalents, of which power installations, both single and two-phase, approximate 15,000 horse-power, covering a wide field of operation. More than 500 elevators are operated from the two-phase power mains.

The service of the Company covers about 150 miles of streets, and occupies 320 miles of duct in the subway system of The Consolidated Telegraph and Electrical Subway Company, with a total of 920 miles of conductor of all classes.

The northern part of the territory supplied by The United Electric Light and Power Company is fraught with historic interest. Back in Revolutionary times it was the scene of a hot conflict afterward known as the Battle of Harlem. General Washington at different times defended certain strategic positions on this rugged part of Manhattan Island. One of the old forts, Fort Washington, still stands, bearing the name of its founder. The famous Jumel Mansion is located at 155th street.

The Bronx Gas and Electric Company

The Bronx Gas and Electric Company covers a territory which has developed with unusual rapidity. When the Company was organized in 1893 with an office in a story and a half wooden shack in the site of the present attractive office building, it was to light the old township of Westchester. And the work was accomplished by means of a few arc lamps.

In 1895 Westchester became a part of Greater New York. A trolley was put through in 1900 and the subway in 1903, with the result that what was then a thinly settled country township has grown into a prosperous suburb.

The Company's territory comprises 16 square miles, with a population of some 30,000; it was only 4,000 back in 1893. By far the greater part of the district is residential, nearly 9,070 commuting into the City. This population is largely transient, houses usually being rented only for the season, and in the case of ownership, the party remaining until the property is sold. There are some few factories and store yards and some mill works, for which this Company supplies light and power.

The power generated during the past year was 2,558,000 kilowatts. This marks an increase in business of something over 5,000% since the Company was established. The biggest seasons were 1905-6, the years, it will be remembered, of the great coal strike. During this time there was an increase in the use of various electrical heating and cooking apparatus, which has to a large extent fallen off since. The new transit facilities doubtless had a great deal to do with the surprising growth of the business through that period. However, the use has continued on the increase, the gain of the past year having been 15%.

The Great White Way, Looking South from 41st Street

The Yonkers Electric Light and Power Company

Should Frederick Philipse, the first lord of the Manor of Philipsburgh, return to his ancient home, the Manor House of Yonkers, what a transformation would meet his eyes! Instead of approaching his stately residence from the river and disembarking from a sailing craft, he would now, perhaps, run up from his office in Wall street via the electrically equipped lines of the New York Central and Hudson River Railroad.

Two hundred years of progress and development have changed Yonkers from a mere hamlet, a collection of the log cabins of pioneers, into a progressive manufacturing city of 85,000 inhabitants. The old manor house, erected in the early part of the Eighteenth Century still stands and has received within its walls many prominent men. It is a long way from the chaise and post to the modern conveyances, but now in the very door yard of his lordship's manor house pass trolley cars and automobiles.

A number of years ago this aristocratic old mansion descended from its exclusive atmosphere and entered upon a political career, becoming the office of the mayor and other city officials. In this capacity it served until the recent opening of a new and imposing City Hall, which is located on a site commanding a beautiful view of the Hudson River and Palisades.

Since 1887, when the Yonkers Light and Power Company opened shops, wonderful advances have been made in the use of electric current. Today there are burning within the city 100,000 incandescent lamps. Electric current is furnished to the small consumer as well as to the occupants of the magnificent residences further back on the beautiful hills, where besides having current for light and power, it is used extensively for heating and cooking. Curiously enough electric household apparatus was widely used in these handsome old houses, before it came into favor among the Manhattanites.

Looking East Along 42d Street from Times Square

TIMES

The Westchester Lighting Company

The Westchester Lighting Company, with its subsidiary companies, supplies all of Westchester County with the exception of Yonkers, with electricity and gas. Westchester County covers some 296,320 acres and has a population of approximately 200,000. The executive offices of the Westchester Lighting Company are at Mount Vernon, but branches have been established in a number of geographical centres and the general distribution work is taken care of from these several points. To facilitate the handling of business, display rooms are located in such centres as Yonkers, Mount Vernon, New Rochelle, Port Chester, White Plains, Tarrytown and Mount Kisco.

The county is developing rapidly and is a most promising field for the lighting industry. The principal electric generating station is situated at New Rochelle. It is a waterside station, located on Echo Bay of Long Island Sound. The capacity of this plant is about 7,600 kilowatts and from it current is transmitted to sub-stations at Mount Vernon, Port Chester, White Plains, Tarrytown and Mount Kisco. Mount Kisco and Tarrytown have emergency steam plants with a total capacity of about 700 kilowatts.

Current is generated entirely by steam, there being no available water power for such a purpose in the County. The Mount Kisco sub-station is tied in with the Ossining power-house of the Northern

Westchester Lighting Company, a subsidiary of the Westchester Company, by means of a high tension transmission line, and can be supplied either from New Rochelle or Ossining, or in case of emergency can generate its own current. This applies also to the Tarrytown sub-station.

Aside from the Peekskill and Ossining equipment, the distribution system consists of 1,700 miles of wire, 17,750 poles and about 2,500 transformers. The street lighting system carries about 1,000 arc and 4,500 tungsten lamps.

The Company is furnishing power for the White Plains, Mamaroneck and Tarrytown Trolley Company, and for the Pittsburg Contracting Company, which is now engaged in building a section of the new Catskill Aqueduct near White Plains. Other "long hour users" on the lines are several of the iron foundries in the City of Port Chester, these making a practically even load throughout the day in the Port Chester district. The district taken as a whole is a residential one. On the Company's books December 31st, 1910, were about 9,000 meters with a connected lighting load of 20,000 kilowatts, approximately 2.2 kilowatts per consumer.

Columbus Circle, Looking South
The light streaks represent the headlights of oncoming trolley cars and automobiles

Waterside Stations

Waterside

—Where is generated that mysterious force which serves to make a city light and clean and livable.

Within sound of the hoarse, dry moan of two gigantic fourteen thousand kilowatt steam turbines, how very far away seems the little Pearl Street Station of eighteen eighty-two, which, with its historical "Jumbos" formed the base for "almost fifteen miles of mains and feeders!"

The present Edison System, covering twenty-one square miles, supplies current on a three-phase system to over ninety-one thousand customers through countless, delicately adjusted meters. And the coal consumption alone, of a plant enormous enough to furnish this amount of power, runs into a total of two thousand tons a day.

Considering such figures as these, it is easily perceived why Waterside with a capacity of five hundred thousand horse-power,—supplying connections to nearly five million lamps,—is today the largest of its kind in the world.

Even against the background of twentieth century understanding, how portentous of an undreamed era are the three copper strands, no thicker than a man's wrist, which leave here to do their part in lighting a city of close on five million souls.

In addition, the Edison System embraces thirty-three sub-stations, six branch offices and a working force of five thousand, who make over five million telephone calls a year in conducting the business of the Company.

Probably no form of modern engineering meets more of the difficult and unexpected as this of illuminating a big centre of industry, where the size of "load" must necessarily always remain an uncontrollable factor.

In recent illustration of this is the afternoon of March second, when occurred a sudden flurry of snow. In the growing dark throughout the city, people simply snapped a button and never gave the matter a second thought. But at Waterside, on the signal of hooting whistles, men jumped in swift and practiced haste to their stations,—for the slender finger of the indicator was rising at the rate of fifty thousand kilowatts in five minutes!

Never for a single moment, did the lights grow dim—which was one of the rewards born of the years of unresting, vigilant alertness these men exert, who work steadfast always confronted with strange, as yet unheard of problems and still, for all a thousand difficulties whose boast it rightly is, that since eighteen eighty-three, except for the brief time taken in the erection of a new station, the current has never left the mains!

The Western Union Telegraph Company

.—— .... .—— .... .—— .... ——. .. —.. .—— ....———. .... —

" What hath God wrought? "

These were the words flashed by Morse from Baltimore to Washington that wonderful day back in 1844, over the first telegraph line ever constructed. Perhaps the mind of the great inventor as he sat at the instrument and ticked off the now famous first message, was piercing the veil of the future, and before his eyes came the momentary vision of the transcendent glories of another century clustering about his invention. Were not these words the inspired utterance of a great dreamer, as to his ears sounded the roar and rumble of the transmission of millions of messages a day? Now that we can view in retrospection the 66 years of marvelous progress of the telegraph industry it would seem that this were so.

During the seven years that followed the construction of the first line more than fifty different telegraph companies sprang up in various parts of the United States. In 1851, however, began the history of The Western Union Telegraph Company, when articles of association of The New York and Mississippi Valley Printing Telegraph Company—the original name of the Company—were filed at Albany. Local consolidations of the various companies in the East followed, and one by one, by lease, by purchase, or by exchange of stock, the companies in the West came into or were absorbed by the new company, which by an act of the New York Legislature in 1856 had its name changed from The New York and Mississippi Valley Printing Telegraph Company to The Western Union Telegraph Company, indicating the union of the Western lines into one compact system.

In 1861, the next important step was taken, when a line was constructed across the plains connecting the Eastern and Western systems. So rapid was the Company's growth in the years that followed, that in the year 1876 there were 18,729,567 messages transmitted over its wires. In 1910 the number of messages sent over the 1,429,049 miles of Western Union wire was 75,135,405, while the Company's receipts for the same year were $33,-889,202.93.

The Sheridan Statue, Central Park

Perhaps the most interesting if not the most important event of recent years in The Western Union was the introduction of the "night letter" and later of the "day letter." The night letter, which has become immensely popular, was instituted to give the public the benefit of the night hours, when business on the lines is light, by sending a fifty-word message at the usual ten-word day rate, subject to delivery in the morning. The day letter can be sent at a lower rate than the regular message, but the message is given the precedence over the day letter. This gives the Company the opportunity of filling in the valleys between its peaks with day letters, keeping its vast force and equipment always busy.

The New York office of the Western Union Telegraph Company, at 195 Broadway, is with one exception, the largest telegraph office in the world.

Broadway, Looking North from Times Square

Looking South from Times Square

Looking North from Times Square

The Postal Telegraph-Cable Company

The thousands of miles of wire which comprise the great system of The Postal Telegraph-Cable Company in the United States have for their focusing point the large and adequately equipped operating room of the Company in the Postal Telegraph Building at 253 Broadway, opposite City Hall, New York. Here they connect with the Atlantic system of the Commercial Cable Company, and radiating from New York, reach every place of importance in the United States, making connection with the Commercial Pacific Cable at San Francisco, and at Montreal with the extensive system of the Canadian Pacific Railway, with which a close working arrangement is maintained.

The trunk line wires are brought into New York from the West under the Hudson River by subaqueous cables, and thence by underground cables to a terminal room in the basement of the Postal Telegraph building. The wires from the North and East are brought under the Harlem River to the same point, and after passing through the necessary protective devices all wires reach the operating room on the twelfth floor, where they are connected directly to the switchboards.

Each switchboard is arranged to contain fifty line wires, which is the maximum number that it is possible for two chief operators to supervise. The switchboards are connected with the various exchanges and branch offices by underground cables.

Directly in front of the switchboards are located the automatic repeaters which perform the function of forwarding through from one wire to another, or from branch offices through to a distant city, without the intervention of receiving or sending operators.

The Postal Telegraph Building was erected specially for telegraph purposes, and its conveniences and arrangements are unexcelled. The wires are operated exclusively by the American Morse system which is upon the simplex, duplex or quadruplex plan, according to the exigencies of the traffic. Chemical batteries, which at one time were exclusively employed for furnishing current for the operation of main wires, have, during the last twenty-five years, been almost entirely replaced by motor generators and transformers. Forty-volt currents are used for all local purposes and for short branch wires in cities. The higher potentials are used for the operation of the apparatus upon the main wires, 200 volts being used for very long, high resistance single circuits, and also for duplexes, while 375 volts is used exclusively in the operation of quadruplexes.

Direct circuits are worked daily from New York to San Francisco, a distance of 3,250 miles; to New Orleans, a distance of 1,334 miles; to St. Louis, a distance of 1,048 miles; to Atlanta, a distance of 882 miles; to Chicago, a distance of 900 miles; and to many other points.

Early Evening, Lower New York

"Cortland,—Twelve Thousand!"

When the late E. H. Harriman once complained that he could not get good service over a certain long-distance line, an expert was sent to inquire into the trouble. On his return, he reported that nothing could be done, as Harriman wanted the impossible.

"Well," said the chief, calmly, "if he wants the impossible, I guess we'll have to give it to him!"

This illustrates the telephone engineer's point of view—a point of view it is given to very few to understand, for looking at the question from the outside, there is little or nothing to suggest the baffling problems, and heavy responsibilities of his profession. Nothing, except a familiar little desk-instrument that can be held in one hand,—but which happens to be the sensitive end of a vast system, embodying some million-one-hundred-thousand-miles of underground wire!

Fifty-four exchanges; five thousand men; six thousand girls, making two million connections a day. Cables, aerials, submarine wires, batteries and intricate switchboards! Could anyone have imagined, that a business of such staggering magnitude was to spring up almost over-night in a single city!

In thirty-five years, it has grown with such strides,—at the rate of almost one hundred telephones a day,—that at present, the New York City Telephone Company alone, is connecting as many instruments as there are in all Great Britain and Germany combined, for nowhere else in the world is there such a metallic nerve-system as among the skyscrapers of Manhattan.

Several hundred experts are continually at work on unwonted problems, and at the present moment these people have strung a line from New York City to Denver, trying to make it carry conversation! It is more than a two-thousand-mile job with a corps of experts through nine states; another impossibility, of course,—but presently it will be done, and then this same crew will push the wire on out to 'Frisco.

They are reaching steadily towards truth, in the great question "What is Electricity?"—and some day they will solve it, just as once before they solved by a marvel of wire-wizardry, that uncanny question of the "phantom circuit," whereon three messages may travel along two pairs of wires.

Always against them, has been pitted the impossible and unknowable, yet they have never wavered in this business of theirs,—the transporting along tiny copper wires a force that is swifter than light, and feebler than a sunbeam.

Looking North Along Fifth Avenue, Union Square

The Interborough Rapid Transit Company

The largest subway system in the world, with its hundreds of miles of track, tunnels under two rivers, and other marvellous engineering feats, together with all of the elevated roads now in operation on Manhattan Island and in the Borough of the Bronx—this is the great Interborough Rapid Transit Company of New York.

Perhaps the most interesting part of the Interborough system is the subway. This is one of the foremost examples of present-day skill and ingenuity, and has demonstrated that underground railroads can be built beneath the congested streets of the city, making possible in the near future a comprehensive system of sub-surface transportation extending throughout the wide territory of Greater New York.

The difficulties confronting the constructors of the subway were well nigh appalling. Towering buildings along the streets had to be considered, the streets themselves were already occupied with a complicated network of sewers, water and gas mains, electric cable conduits, electric surface railway conduits, telegraph and power conduits, and vaults from the abutting buildings extended under the streets.

The completed subway is a tribute to the master mind of its builder the late John B. McDonald. For a five-cent fare it is possible to ride from Brooklyn to either Van Cortlandt or Bronx Park or to any intermediate point. There is a separate express service, with its own tracks, and the stations are so arranged that passengers may pass from local trains to express trains, and vice versa, without delay and without payment of additional fare.

Special precautions have been taken to prevent a failure of the electric power and the consequent delays of traffic. An electro-pneumatic block signal system has been devised which excels any previous system, and is unique in its mechanism.

The third rail for conveying the electric current is covered, so as to prevent injury to passengers and employees from contact. Special emergency and fire alarm signal systems are installed throughout the length of the road. At a few stations, where the road is not near the surface, escalators and elevators are provided.

The power house for the subway is located at Fifty-ninth street and the North River and has a capacity of approximately 100,000 horse-power. It covers an area of 190,792 square feet. The capacity of the coal bunkers at this station is 18,000 tons. The boiler room contains seventy-two boilers arranged in pairs or batteries. The power for the operation of elevated trains is generated at Seventy-fifth street and the East River. The area there is 114,340 square feet, while its capacity is 64,000 horse-power.

The New Public Library Building
Fifth Avenue from 41st to 42d Streets

The Brooklyn Rapid Transit

It was once said of an ancient imperial city that all roads lead to Rome; with equal verity, at least in the Summer season, this epigram might be varied to read: "All trolley cars run to Coney Island." As a place of fun and frolic, mirth and laughter, a rapid, strenuous, dashing, whirling, hurly-burly of noise, brilliant, hetrogeneous, unconventional, eminently human, crowded by day and night, it responds to the elemental call of man for diversion.

Out of sixteen routes from Brooklyn and Manhattan to Coney Island, thirteen are owned and operated by The Brooklyn Rapid Transit. Over this baker's dozen of lines some twelve hundred six-car trains are operated in a single busy Summer's day—in addition to a sixty-second headway of trolley cars on six surface car routes.

It is no unusual task for The Brooklyn Rapid Transit to carry a quarter of a million persons on the ten mile trip down to Coney Island in the morning and early afternoon—then to bring this whole cityfull home at nightfall. The Culver terminal, at Coney Island, is the largest railroad terminal in the world which has but three months of real service throughout the year.

To operate this station requires unusual drill and discipline on the part of the men of The Brooklyn Rapid Transit. Three men are constantly on duty in the interlocking tower that protects the elevated train operation in the terminal—a small regiment guards the platforms, exits and entrances—and all of these men have brought both skill and experience to the execution of their difficult tasks.

To carry this great tide of pleasure-seeking humanity on its flow to Coney Island and to Brighton, to bring it safely home upon the ebb is a master task for the power resources of The Brooklyn Rapid Transit. This task has almost equalled the Company's record load—carrying homebound Christmas shoppers, in addition to heating and lighting the cars in which they rode—a load that took 144,000 horse-power in a single hour of a December evening. To meet the power necessities of summertime at Coney Island, a transforming station is maintained as part of the equipment of Culver terminal. Four 1,000 k. w. units form the mechanical equipment of this modern station.

The Brooklyn Rapid Transit, with its 568 miles of surface and elevated lines is probably the largest single city railroad in the world. The fact that the longest of these lines is less than fourteen miles only goes to show the remarkable density of the system. Over these lines 3,000 surface and elevated cars are sent each day—the total mileage of Brooklyn surface cars in the course of twenty-fours is equal to a distance six times around the world at the equator.

Public Service Electric Company of New Jersey

No single electric lighting company serves a larger territory than does Public Service Electric Company of New Jersey. This corporation, whose home office is in Newark, serves an area embracing twelve counties and one hundred and fifty-seven municipalities, in which live more than two million people, nearly four-fifths of the population of the entire State.

Public Service Electric Company was incorporated in July, 1910, taking over all the electrical business of Public Service Corporation, which came into existence in 1903. It controlled almost all the electric, gas and street railway business of the northern and central parts of the State.

The first electric lighting in New Jersey was done by the Newark Electric Light and Power Company in 1884, two years after the company's organization.

The territory of this early company was confined to three blocks on Broad Street and about seven on Market Street, where some of the business men were induced to use current for lighting their premises.

The growth of the electrical business is shown by comparative figures of 1903 and December 31, 1910. In 1903 there were fourteen generating stations, now there are twenty-eight; there were 156 generators with a capacity of 40,075 kilowatts, now there are 189 generators with a capacity of 124,158 kilowatts. In 1903 there were produced

129,614,180 kilowatt hours; in 1910, 288,740,147 kilowatt hours. There were 47 miles of transmission lines and 25 miles of conduits in 1903, while now there are 374 miles of transmission lines and 79 miles of conduits. The total commercial load connected at the earlier date was 710,000 50-watt equivalents, as against 2,613,236 50-watt equivalents in 1910.

Looking South from Times Tower

South Beach, Staten Island

A Terrace View in Yonkers

The Palisades at Yonkers

Dredging Boat on the Hudson, Yonkers

The Hall of Fame

High Bridge

Astoria

Canarsie

JEROME MYERS
1911

5¢

Index

www.ingramcontent.com/pod-product-compliance
Lightning Source LLC
LaVergne TN
LVHW010607110826
845149LV00003B/801

* 9 7 8 1 4 1 8 1 8 7 3 3 0 *